Dear mouse friends,
Welcome to the world of

# Geronimo Stilton

THE RODENT'S GAZETTE
EDITORIAL STAFF

**Geronimo Stilton**
A learned and brainy mouse; editor of *The Rodent's Gazette*

**Thea Stilton**
Geronimo's sister and special correspondent at *The Rodent's Gazette*

**Trap Stilton**
An awful joker; Geronimo's cousin and owner of the store Cheap Junk for Less

**Benjamin Stilton**
A sweet and loving nine-year-old mouse; Geronimo's favorite nephew

Geronimo Stilton

# GARBAGE DUMP DISASTER

Scholastic Inc.

Published by Scholastic Inc., *Publishers since 1920*, 557 Broadway, New York, NY 10012. SCHOLASTIC and associated logos are trademarks and/or registered trademarks of Scholastic Inc.



ISBN 978-93-5471-023-0

Text by Geronimo Stilton
Original title *Lo strano caso del ladro di spazzatura*
Cover by Iacopo Bruno, Giuseppe Facciotto, and Christian Aliprandi
Graphic designer: Pietro Piscitelli/theWorldofDOT
Illustrations by Giuseppe Facciotto, Carolina Livio, Diaria Cerchi, and Valeria Cairoli
Translated by Anna Pizzelli
Special thanks to Anna Bloom
Interior design by Becky James

First printing 2021
This reprint edition, November 2024

Printed in India by Saurabh Printers Pvt. Ltd.

# Something Stinks!

I **tossed** and turned in bed. The night air was hotter than the inside of a grilled cheese. I counted cats, I stared at the moon, I tried listening to a podcast about the history of Parmesan. Just as I finally drifted off to sleep, a **LOUD** noise jolted me awake.

Ring, ring, ring!

**Holy cheese**, I had to get to the office! I am *Geronimo Stilton*, the editor-in-chief of *The Rodent's Gazette*, the most **famouse** newspaper on Mouse Island.

I rushed to the office and sat at my desk. I quickly drank my **cheddar kale smoothie** and got to work on my latest article. Deep in thought, I barely noticed when the door to my office **squeaked** open.

But I did notice a strange **SMELL**. In fact, it was hard not to notice! The smell was really more of a **big stink**. Or a big stinky stench. What was that?

Without looking up from my computer, I held my nose with my paw. "**Rotten Gorgonzola**, who's there?"

A familiar snout peeked through the door. The snout was familiar and so was the banana-yellow overcoat . . .

Standing before me was none other than my friend and Mouse Island's most *famouse* private detective, **Hercule Poirat**!

But then I noticed something slightly odd. Hercule had a

clothespin perched right on the end of his snout!

He started talking a mile a minute. "Beronimo, canyoudoobeeabavor?"

I waved my paws to get him to STOP. "Slow down, Hercule! I can't understand a Parmesan-dusted thing you are saying!"

He started over, LOUDER and slower this time. "Beronimo. Can you doo bee a baaaaaaavooooor. Bits urgent!!"

My WHISKERS shook with impatience. "Hercule! I have no idea what you're saying. I don't have time for this. I'm working on a very important fondue article!"

Hercule let out a squeak of surprise and pointed a paw at the clothespin on his snout.

He removed it and started over. "There! Can you understand me now?"

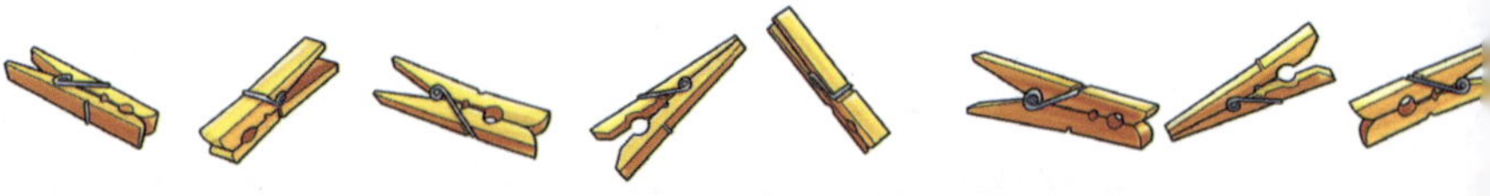

I nodded wearily.

"Great! Because I need you to do me a favor! It's urgent!" He clasped his PAWS together.

I sighed. "Twisted cat tails! Every time you visit, it's because you need something. And it's always very urgent."

Hercule just grinned at me in response. Reluctantly, I gave him my full attention.

"Okay, what's so urgent? And why are you wearing a clothespin? And why do you smell so terrible?" I said, sniffling.

Hercule leaped toward my desk and pulled a tissue out of his overcoat pocket. With it came an avalanche of clothespins.

"Geronimo, something in New Mouse City stinks worse than rotten Gorgonzola. And I'm not talking about this smell. I'm talking about — a thief!"

"A thief?" I repeated. "What are they **stealing**?"

"That's just it, Geronimo. That is the strangest thing about the whole case. This rascally rodent is stealing . . ." He paused dramatically.

I rolled my eyes.

"The thief is stealing **GARBAGE**!" Hercule cried.

I gasped.

"That's why I stink. I've been up all night sorting through dumpsters," he said while he clacked his clothespin at me.

I shuddered. "Who would want to steal trash?"

**WHO, WHO, WHO?**

Just then my sister, Thea, walked in, holding her snout with a paw.

"When was the last time either one of you

rats took a shower? Your office stinks like an old bag of shredded cheese that's been left out in the sun."

I groaned.

Hercule stood up a little straighter and moved away from Thea. "So sorry about the SMELL, Thea. That's the scent of a very important investigation!" He puffed out his

chest. "Help me convince Geronimo to join me in finding a crafty trash thief!"

"COOL!" Thea said. "That could be an interesting story for *The Rodent's Gazette*!"

I didn't like the sound of that. Before I could make up an excuse to escape my office, Thea was hustling me up out of my chair.

"Come on, Geronimo, we have to investigate!" She put her camera in the pocket of her jacket.

"Oh, sugar-crusted cheese curds! Thank you, Thea!" Hercule squeaked. "How can I ever thank you enough —"

"By talking less, and getting cracking on this investigation!" Thea interrupted.

I tried to sit back down. "I have a lot of cheese on my plate right now, guys. I think I better stay," I said.

"This is more important!" Thea shook her snout at me.

"Fine," I grumbled.

"Yay!" Thea cheered. She grabbed my arm and practically pulled me out the office door.

"We're doing this!" Hercule cried. "Let's go catch that thief!"

# SCENE OF THE GRIME

We all hopped into Hercule's BANANAMOBILE. Hercule took off like a **rocket**. Our whiskers ***BLEW*** in the wind. I held a paw to my stomach. I don't like going fast.

Hercule started to explain how he'd gotten

the case. "New Mouse City's mayor, Frederick Fuzzypaws, called me yesterday. He said that a lot of **trash** from the new recycling plant had disappeared **OVERNIGHT**. No one could explain how it had happened."

Hercule turned a corner, and a **SMELLY** breeze blew past our snouts, announcing our destination before we even saw the sign: **NEW MOUSE CITY EXPERIMENTAL RECYCLING PLANT**.

RECYCLING COLLECTION
1. PLASTIC COLLECTION
2. GLASS COLLECTION
3. PAPER AND CARDBOARD COLLECTION
4. METAL COLLECTION
5. ELECTRONICS COLLECTION
6. BULK ITEM COLLECTION
7. OIL COLLECTION
8. RUBBLE COLLECTION
9. WOOD AND TRIMMINGS COLLECTION
10. ORGANIC WASTE COLLECTION
11. PARKING
12. OFFICE
11
12

5
6
4
7
3
2
8
9

Hercule came to a stop in front of the **guard booth**. The uniformed mouse there stepped out and held up his PAW.

"No entry without official authorization! There was a **THEFT** last night, and only employees are allowed in today."

Hercule showed the guard his private detective badge and **winked**. "I have been sent by Mayor Fuzzypaws himself to investigate the robbery! I have a meeting with the recycling plant's manager. My team has **special** permission to be on the grounds."

The guard went back into his booth and made a call. Before long, he raised the barrier and **waved** us through. "Good luck!" he called.

What we saw inside was incredimouse. Heaps and heaps of all kinds of trash were piled everywhere: plastic, aluminum, paper, and organic waste — the stinkiest of it all!

Hercule steered the BANANAMOBILE into a parking spot. We all HOPPED out.

"Over here," Hercule called. He waved a paw and led us over to one of the GARBAGE collection stations. "See that empty space there? This area is normally full to the brim. This is where last night's trash was stolen from. It's an ENORMOUSE amount to get away with." He looked confused.

Next to me, Thea snapped pictures. Reluctantly, I took my paw off my nose and started jotting down some observations. The STENCH was unbearable!

Poor me . . . My head started to spin . . . Thea noticed and pinched my tail to distract me.

"Geronimo! What's

**wrong**? Don't you dare faint on us."

Hercule started **fanning** me with his paws. "Uh-oh. I think he's going to faint! **Quick**, let's get him inside!"

My head **throbbed**, and my vision **DARKENED**. "Good night!" I squeaked before finally fainting.

When I came to, I was lying on a soft **sofa** in the recycling plant's office, a **COLD** cloth on my snout.

"Poor you, you have a little bit of heatstroke," a gentle voice whispered. "Are you feeling any better now, Mr. Stilton?"

**Slowly**, I tilted up my snout and saw

a kind-looking rodent. She had HONEY-COLORED fur and a long dark braid down her back, held together by a GREEN hairclip in the shape of a LEAF.

"Yes, thanks," I said. "But I must be late! We're supposed to be having a meeting with someone named Fontal — the manager of the plant."

The mouse in front of me smiled. "Well, you're in luck — that's me! I'm Ms. Fontal, manager of New Mouse City Experimental Recycling Plant!"

She pointed a paw at the name badge on her lab coat.

"Welcome, Mr. Stilton! I do hope you can help solve our garbage mystery!"

# TRASH TOUR

Ms. Fontal helped me up and led me back out into a **WAITING** room, where Hercule and Thea were standing.

Thea rushed over to me. "Are you feeling any better, little brother?" she asked. "It was brutally HOT out there. We could have fried a grilled cheese on the pavement!"

Hercule snorted. "I told him to use the clothespin, but Geronimo would not hear it! Next time maybe he will take my advice."

I ignored him and turned back to the plant manager. "I don't think I properly introduced myself, Ms. Fontal. My name is Gilton, Steronimo Gilton."

Hercule and Thea burst out **laughing**.

I started to **SWEAT**. "Um, I mean, Stilton, Geronimo Stilton. I am the editor-in-chief of *The Rodent's Gazette*."

Ms. Fontal **laughed** and held out a paw to **shake**. "Mr. Stilton, no need to introduce yourself, I already know who you are. I read your paper every day."

A fan! How **mousetastic**!

## FLORA FONTAL

**WHO:** A brilliant scientist.
**HER PASSION:** Protecting the environment.
**HER DREAM:** Slow the pace of climate change.
**HER JOB:** She was appointed manager of the Experimental Recycling Plant to help improve New Mouse City's recycling program.
**ASSISTED BY:** Randall Crumb.
**PERSONAL LIFE:** She likes sailing, hiking, and riding her bicycle.
**SPECIAL TALENTS:** She is an excellent chef and an amazing baker. Her cheese tiramisu is mouserific!

"It's always nice to meet someone who likes my work. But please, call me Geronimo." My fur blushed **Pink**.

"Of course, Geronimo! And you must call me **Flora**!"

"Are you getting a little flustered?" Hercule asked.

I groaned and elbowed him in the side. "**Moldy mozzarella**, will you shut your snout!"

I always get a little shy when I meet new mice! Plus, Flora is so smart — and she likes my articles!

Thea **scrolled** through the photos on her camera that she had taken so far. "Now that we've all been introduced, where should we **start** our investigation?"

"We're just waiting for my assistant. Oh, here he is now!"

A young ratlet wearing a white lab coat walked into the office. His **BADGE** read RANDALL CRUMB.

"How can I HELP?" he asked.

## RANDALL CRUMB

WHO: Expert in recycling technology, recently hired at the Experimental Recycling Plant to assist Ms. Fontal.
WORK HISTORY: In order to hire the best expert, New Mouse City held a contest, and Randall Crumb was the winner. He holds seven degrees: chemistry, physics, math, biology, medicine, engineering, and environmental science. In short, he knows everything about everything!
PERSONALITY: He is very shy, and he seems to be quite a private rodent.

# TALKING TRASH

Randall was tall and thin, with a pointy snout and frizzy whiskers, fur buzzed short, and a pair of metal frame glasses.

He timidly offered Flora a bunch of RED roses. "I, uh, found these outside and thought you would like them."

I scrunched up my snout. Found them? That didn't seem likely.

Flora put the flowers in a vase. "Well, that's KIND of you, Randall. I'm actually allergic, but it's the thought that counts."

Randall's snout FELL a little, but when he

realized Hercule, Thea, and I were all staring at him, he plastered on a WEAK smile.

"Oh, hello. You must be the famouse Geronimo Stilton, editor-in-chief of *The Rodent's Gazette*." He held out a PAW for me to shake. "What an honor to have a famouse journalist and author at the plant!" He was being very polite, but I could see in his eyes that he wasn't pleased to have me here.

BUT WHY? It seemed like he had a crush on Flora. And she was a big fan of mine. Could that be it?

Thea offered her PAW as well. "Nice to meet you, Randall Crumb. We're impressed by the size of the operation here."

"There's more garbage in this dump than you can shake a cheese straw at!" Hercule said.

"Uh, yes, indeed. But this is not a **dump**," Randall said, annoyed. "It's a state-of-the-art experimental recycling facility. I'm helping Flora totally **revamp** the recycling program in New Mouse City. Eventually,

we hope it will be a GLOBAL model for sustainability."

"How marvemouse!" I exclaimed. "I can't wait to see more of it."

"As long as you don't faint again," Thea mumbled.

I ignored her and continued. "Well, so far, it seems very organized."

Just then Flora began passing out plates. "Before we get started with the tour, I thought we could all use a quick snack while I run through some recycling basics with you. This is my specialty: cheesy tiramisu."

She took a heart-shaped cheese tiramisu out of a small refrigerator she kept in her office and started cutting it into SLICES. Then

she sat down at her computer and pulled up a RECYCLING presentation.

As we **happily** munched, Flora grinned around the room. "Thank you so much for coming to help us. We're so close to completely reimagining the **GARBAGE** collection and disposal system here in New Mouse City. I'd hate for anything to get in the way of that."

"Of course!" I squeaked. "It will be easy-cheesy!"

Now we just had to figure out what was really going on here!

Yummy!

## SEPARATING WASTE

At New Mouse City Experimental Recycling Plant, we are in charge of collecting and recycling all kinds of trash, using different methods and techniques. Recycling can only succeed if everyone works together: recycling starts in everyone's homes and on the streets.

In your own home, you can dispose of your trash in different kinds of bins: (1) organic food waste, (2) paper, (3) plastic, (4) glass, (5) mixed waste (this is trash that cannot be recycled, for example, greasy containers, broken toys, toothbrushes, diapers, etc.).

In public places, you might have the option to dispose of trash in a few different kinds of containers, too: ones for paper, plastic, glass, organic food waste, or special trash.

Certain trash has to be disposed of at designated recycling centers. For example: batteries, electronics, and certain kinds of oils and bulky items (like tree branches and construction debris).

A lot of times, unfortunately, all trash is disposed of in the same bin. But this can cause problems at recycling plants. If there are separate bins for different kinds of trash available, it's important to follow the directions.

# A TRASH TOUR

After Flora's presentation, we all went outside. The sun was no longer high in the sky, and the air was slightly cooler. We walked through the entire plant with Flora and Randall.

Flora described what each section of the

plant was responsible for. She was more enthusiastic about GARBAGE than any other rodent I had ever met!

Thea paused in her relentless picture taking to ask Flora a question. "What kind of trash did the thief take, anyway? Was it some kind of special garbage?"

Flora shook her snout. "Not really. Most of the GARBAGE taken was from the organic food waste section."

Hercule stuck his tongue out. "What in the name of cheese toasties is the rascally rat going to do with a bunch of rotting banana peels?"

I shrugged. "Who knows?" I jotted down some notes in my book.

"Can we go back to the scene of the crime?" Hercule asked.

"Of course!" Flora said.

We followed her back through the PLANT and to the organic food waste area.

Hercule leaned over the railing to peer at the enormouse hole in the trash that had been left behind by the thief. He seemed somehow not to mind the SMELL.

Moldy mozzarella, this was the stinkiest job we'd ever taken on!

"There must be tons of food waste missing! I have to get a CLOSER look!"

"Ugh, really?" I asked, **groaning**.

Thea rolled her eyes at me and motioned for me to follow them down to the **GARBAGE** collection floor.

"Hmm," Hercule said. "This is supposed to be the area for organic food waste, but there are a lot of crushed plastic bottles

## WHAT IS ORGANIC WASTE?

Organic waste can be composed of a variety of things, including leftover cooked and uncooked food, fish bones, animal bones, dried fruit, eggshells, dirt and gardening trash, pieces of wood, ashes, coal, matches, tea and coffee grounds, greasy paper, and paper napkins.

The best way to dispose of organic waste and transform it into a useful material is through the composting process. It is very important to make sure that trash that would impede this process (such as liquids, metal, glass, porcelain, pottery, medicine, and gauze) is not collected with organic waste.

around. Is that normal?" He turned to look at Flora.

"It's not," she said. "We try to keep all the **trash** as separated as

possible." She frowned.

"Did anyone **hear** or **SEE** the thief?" Thea asked. "Maybe he **flew** in? I don't see any tire tracks on the ground. How else

would a rodent make off with this much GARBAGE?" She gestured around with her paw and then took a few more pictures.

Flora shook her snout. "I don't remember hearing any engine noise or seeing any flying vehicles. There was a FULL MOON, so it was very bright."

Hercule closed his eyes. His whiskers shook slightly. I could tell that he was concentrating hard on this new piece of information. What a mysterimouse case!

"Strange . . . Holey Swiss cheese, it's weird that the thief would plan a job for the night of a FULL MOON, when it's bright and therefore so much easier to be seen. It just doesn't add up!"

# CLUES COLLECTED SO FAR:

1. There are no **car** or **truck** tire tracks around the hole.
2. The thief might have arrived from above, on some sort of **flying vehicle**.
3. No one heard anything **odd**, so the vehicle must be very **quiet**.
4. No one saw anything **odd**, so the vehicle must be a very **stealthy**. Or invisible!
5. The vehicle is powerful, able to lift an **enormouse amount of trash**.
6. The thief **left behind** flattened plastic bottles.
7. Interesting detail: The theft occurred during a **full moon**, not a great time for a heist, since it is not completely dark.

# Cabbage Leaves and Apple Cores

After our last stop at the organic waste section, we all promised to return the next day. We needed a good night's sleep to CRACK this cheesy crouton of a mystery. I was so tired from the day's trip that I didn't even need to count cheese wheels to fall asleep.

The next morning, I was RUDELY awoken by a loud ringing sound.

Ring, ring, ring!

Groggy, I turned off my alarm clock.

Ring, ring, ring!

But the noise didn't stop.

Just then I heard banging on my front door.

"Geronimo!" Hercule shouted. "Why are

you not answering your doorbell?!"

"Come open the door!" Thea cried.

CRUSTY CAT TAILS! What were they doing here at this hour?

Quickly, I pulled on my clothes and dashed downstairs.

"What?!" I shouted, opening the door.

"There's been another theft! At a canned food factory!" Thea said, breathlessly.

They didn't have to say anything else. I shut the door behind me and started jogging toward Hercule's Bananamobile. "Let's shake our tails!" I said.

The traffic was heavy, but finally we made it to our destination: a canned food factory called VegFruit. The factory was housed in an enormouse GREEN building, with pictures of fruits and vegetables painted on the outside of it.

Waiting outside the factory entrance stood Mayor Fuzzypaws himself. If the mayor was here, this must mean the latest trash theft was **big**.

"Hello, hello!" the mayor boomed. "I'm so glad you are all here now. We need all paws on deck to nose out the rascally rat who is stealing our **GARBAGE**!"

Hercule's snout turned serious. "Never fear, Mr. Mayor. We will root out the rotten cheese slice among us! I have some theories, but it's too early to share them."

I frowned. What theories? He certainly hadn't shared them with us.

Before I could ask Hercule, the mayor introduced us to the factory owner, Veg Tables.

Hercule got right to business. "Tell us what happened, Mr. Tables."

Mr. Tables led us to a **LARGE** area behind the factory. "Yesterday we finished production on a large quantity of **apple** and **WATERMELON JAM**. We also produced a large amount of sauerkraut. At the end of the day, we gathered all the fruit and vegetable **scraps** in this area. They're left in the open air to decompose a bit before we take them out via truck. But when the trucks arrived this morning, the whole lot of **scraps** had disappeared."

Hercule's whiskers **TWITCHED**. "Hmmm. I assume no one **SAW** or **heard** anything, correct?"

Mr. Tables shook his snout. "The night guard says he did not SEE or hear anything, even though the moon was full and bright. He did point out one strange thing, though. There are a lot of flattened plastic BOTTLES all around the theft area."

Piles of apple cores and rotten watermelon

rinds still lay scattered around the storage area. Ugh, what a **stench**. We had to hurry up and solve this case before I had to **SMELL** any more garbage!

# The Smell Thickens

The next day, Hercule and Thea arrived at my door first thing in the morning. We sat at my breakfast nook eating fontina scones and cheddar leaf tea, discussing the case.

"I just don't understand what the thief is doing with all that GARBAGE!" Thea said.

I shook my snout. There wasn't an easy explanation yet.

Just then Hercule's cell phone started to ring. He calls it the bananaphone because it is bright yellow and shaped like a BANANA. Hercule says this way he won't lose track of it.

But it just kept ringing!

"What could I have done with it?" Hercule

wondered. Thea and I rolled our eyes.

"Ahhh, there it is! Right in my pocket!"

He pulled out his strange-looking phone. "Hello, Hercule Poirat here. May I ask who's squeaking?"

Hercule listened for a minute. "No! Really?" Hercule said. "Mustard-crusted

cat tails! Okay, we'll be there as soon as we can."

He ended the call and turned to us. "That was Mayor Fuzzypaws. Last night, another theft occurred! It's the same story, but this time, over at the fish market in the center of town."

I wrinkled my snout. This was going to be the stinkiest crime scene yet!

Hercule continued. "The style of the theft exactly matches the previous ones. Only GARBAGE was taken. This time, it was fish bones. No rodent saw or heard even a squeak. And as before, the thief left behind a bunch of flattened plastic bottles."

Thea wiped scone crumbs from her whiskers and stood up. "Well, what are we waiting for? Let's go check it out!"

By the time we arrived at the fish market,

More plastic bottles!
Ugh, the smell!

it was already past noon and the heat was overwhelming. The smell of **fish** was also overwhelming! Rancid rat tales, I could not wait for this investigation to be over.

"Let's make this quick, Hercule," I urged. "I don't know how long I can take this **smell**."

"You can't rush investigative brilliance, Geronimo!" Hercule said. He picked up a fish skeleton. "By now, we know that this thief is very fond of trash. We also know that he needs a lot of it, for some reason. **Organic waste trash** from the recycling plant, spoiled vegetables and fruit, now rotten fish. And he or she always leaves behind a large number of plastic bottles! It's all very STRANGE."

Thea and I nodded. This was a very confusing mystery.

Suddenly, Hercule gasped. "I know!" he cried. "What we need to do is catch our rascally rat with his paw in the cheddar chip cookie jar!"

When Hercule saw the confused looks on our snouts, he continued.

"What we need to do is set a trap!"

# A Mousetrap!

Hercule stalked back and forth and laid out his **PLAN** for us. "For a good trap, you need good bait. In this case — garbage, and lots of it!" He rubbed his snout with one of his paws. "I bet a thousand bananas the thief will show up in no time!"

Then he turned to me and Thea. "This afternoon, you'll put out a special edition of *The Rodent's Gazette*. In it will be a story about an **ENORMOUSE** container of trash stored in New Mouse City's port, ready to be shipped out by boat."

"There is?" I asked.

"No, Cheddarhead! We're making that up! But the thief will think there really

is a mountain of trash ready for the taking!"

Thea and I rushed back to the office and put out the special edition, just as Hercule had suggested. The trap for the trash thief was set!

Now all we had to do was wait. I headed home to work on my fondue article some more.

Back at my desk, I pulled out my notes and sat down at my computer. But **fur-crusted cheese curds**! I had forgotten that my nice new laptop was out for repair. I rested my snout in my paws. What terrible timing. My laptop was a gift from the famouse inventor Beaker Poirat (Hercule's cousin!). It's called **CompStar**, and it is a beautiful pistachio green. It's a state-of-the-art prototype that is so intelligent, it functions almost like a robot.

CompStar can even **speak**. It is very efficient and friendly, and I have become **very fond** of it!

I had returned CompStar to Beaker for an update. I **called** him, hoping it was ready by now. "Hi, Beaker, it's Stilton, Geronimo Stilton, speaking. I really need my

## BEAKER POIRAT

Genius inventor. He has a master's degree in comparative engineering. He has invented a few time machines and CompStar, a new type of computer that acts like a robot.

CompStar back. Have you updated its software yet? When can I have it back?"

"You miss CompStar, don't you?" Beaker asked. "I am so happy to hear that. It means my invention is useful to you! CompStar isn't ready yet, but it did want to say hello."

Suddenly, I heard CompStar's voice: "Hi, *Geronimo*, did I hear you miss me? I am so happy to hear that! I miss you, too, Cheddarhead!"

I laughed. "I'm working on a big article, so I could really use you right about now. I'm also helping Hercule investigate an important case about the environment."

"Oh, the environment,"

**CompStar** said. "Don't be a **worryrat**, I will come home soon. Beaker is adding special sense-of-humor software, so soon I will be able to tell you all kinds of jokes!"

**Oh dear.** I wasn't sure I liked the sound of that.

What did Hercule say to the cheese thief?

You've been up to no Gouda!

# COMPSTAR

Invented by Beaker Poirat, it is Geronimo's new prototype computer. Its real name is C3582CTPQR110, but Beaker calls it CompStar, which is much easier to say.

ABOUT COMPSTAR:

It is pistachio green, which is Beaker's favorite color.

It is completely eco-friendly: it is made of recycled plastic mixed with pistachio shells.

It is fueled by pistachio power. Fermented pistachios are concentrated and stored in a special battery that lasts a year.

It has many special functions and behaves just like a robot. For example, it can speak all the languages in the world. If connected to a vehicle, it can drive . . . and it can even order extra-cheesy pizza!

It has two mechanical arms, each with mechanical hands, that allow it to handle objects — and bake cookies!

NOTE: Because it is still a prototype, it is easily upset. It's been known to mope, turn itself to sleep mode, and refuse to turn back on!

# A SHADOW IN THE NIGHT

The next morning, all New Mouse City's residents saw the **news** on the front page of *The Rodent's Gazette* special edition:

**Large Container of Trash Delivered to New Mouse City's Port**

In my office, Hercule **JUMPED** for joy. "Our mousetrap is set! I can't wait to nab this trash thief!"

He handed Thea and me each a **black jumpsuit**, together with matching gloves and ski masks. "This way we can hide in the shadows and wait for the thief to show up! Off we go!"

I felt ridicumouse wearing the jumpsuit. "Are you sure this is necessary?" I squeaked.

"Of course, cheese for brains!" Hercule said. "Now the only thing left for you to do is to call Flora and ask her to meet us at the port."

"F-F-F-Flora?" I stammered. "Why does she need to meet us?"

"She's an environmental expert, that's why! Come on, Geronimo! Don't be a scaredy-mouse. We need all paws on deck."

But still I hesitated. I didn't want to bother her.

Hercule wouldn't take NO for an answer. "We need her there, and she's such a big fan of yours. If you ask, she'll definitely come!"

I sighed. He had me cornered like a rat. I wanted to solve this case. Mostly so we could stop hanging out near garbage all the time . . . And Flora did know so much about trash and environmental issues. "Fine, fine," I said. "I will call and ask her to help us!"

I dialed Flora's number, but as soon as she picked up, it was like a CAT had got my tongue. "Hi, Stilton, it is me, Flora. Wait. You are Flora; I am Stilton. I mean Geronimo." What was I even saying?

Thea rolled her eyes and grabbed my cell phone from my PAWS. "Flora, it's

Thea Stilton. We have planned a **SECRET MISSION** to catch the trash thief, and we need your help. Can you meet us at *The Rodent's Gazette* office within an hour, okay? I'll text you the address. See you soon!"

As soon as Flora joined us, we set out for the port. **NIGHT** had fallen, and we were nearly **invisible** under the cover of darkness. Once there, we hid in a dumpster and waited for the thief to show up.

We waited and waited and waited and

waited. It seemed as if we were waiting for the LONGEST time, until, finally . . .

We heard a noise that sounded like a big a GUST of wind. But the noise got louder and louder, like something was coming closer to our hiding spot. But what? We looked up and stared at the SKY.

As we watched, a LARGE shape crossed in front of the moon. It seemed to be a vehicle of some sort, but it was like no flying vehicle I had ever seen before.

What was it?

What is that?

# A Masked Mouse

The strange-looking flying vehicle quietly got closer and closer. The engine, if it had one, sounded more like a windstorm than an airplane.

It got closer and closer to the ground until it landed right by us.

We leaned around the dumpster to get a better look. GREAT GOBS OF GREASY MOZZARELLA! That wasn't an airplane. It was an enormouse BLIMP, in the shape of a plastic water BOTTLE!

This is why no one had reported seeing anything. The BLIMP was quiet as a mouse and crystal clear. The engine, propellers, and cockpit all seemed to be made of transparent plastic. Even the instrument panel inside the BLIMP seemed to be made out of clear plastic.

Inside the cockpit, we could just make out the shape of a rodent. We saw him switch off the BLIMP and hop out onto the pavement. I gasped, and Thea elbowed me in the ribs. But I couldn't help it! The rodent was wearing a plastic suit of some kind that made him look like a giant GREEN water bottle.

"Look at all this amazing trash!" he whispered. "This is exactly what I need for my next experiment . . ."

Before he even finished talking, Hercule jumped up and let out a squeak. "Stop, trash thief! That's it, we caught you red-pawed!"

The BLIMP pilot slowly turned our way.

It was hard to make out the expression on his snout under his giant **GREEN** helmet.

"Oh dear," he said. "I, uh, hmm."

Thea stepped out as well. "Remove your helmet, Cheddarsnout! Show yourself!"

**Slowly**, he reached his paws up and took his helmet off.

All of our snouts dropped.

"It's you!" I cried.

Standing before us was . . .

**Randall Crumb!**

Flora and I joined Thea and Hercule. Flora looked confused and disappointed. "I don't understand," she said. "Randall, why would you go to all this **trouble** to steal **GARBAGE**? And why would you take it from our

facility? If you had wanted to run some kind of special project, we could have talked about it."

"Oh, well, but — it's only trash!" Randall tried to explain.

"But it wasn't yours to take," Hercule said.

Thea squinted her eyes. "Why, Randall? What is all that trash for?"

Randall shrugged. "Because I knew you wouldn't understand."

Thea frowned. "Try us. I'm pretty sure we will."

"Give us a chance, at least," Flora urged.

He sighed. "It's a LONG STORY. I'll start at the beginning."

We all gathered around to hear what he had to say.

"It all started when I was just a young **mouselet**. I never asked my parents for new toys. I was always **happy** to build **toys** on my own, using wood and cardboard, tin and rubber, or paper and

glue. Any material I could find, really. My friends would bring me their BROKEN dolls, and I would make repairs for them! Soon, I was fixing bigger, more complex things: bicycles, skates, skateboards. I was really good! I saved many things that might otherwise have just been thrown away. Rodents even said I had a special gift for repairing things."

Flora nodded her snout. "Go on," she said.

"I decided to become a SCIENTIST in order to dedicate my life to recycling and saving the planet. I studied hard, and when I attended college, I was able to get seven degrees,

all at the same time, in chemistry, physics, math, biology, medicine, engineering, and

**environmental science!**

"Wow," Thea said.

"Over time, I became more and more **passionate** about saving the environment.

"That's when I met Flora. I felt like somebody finally understood my work and my interests." He smiled ruefully. "I have to admit, I had a little **crush**." He shot a look at Flora.

Thea was getting impatient. "That's a wonderful story, but what about the trash?" she cried.

# Plastic — It's Fantastic!

Randall's whiskers trembled. "Oh, of course. As I was saying, after college, I became a researcher. I set up my own SECRET laboratory on a hill near New Mouse City. I started work on a machine that could generate energy using trash that would otherwise end up in a landfill."

"But how marvemouse!" Flora squeaked. "Why didn't you ever tell me about that?"

Randall shrugged. "It seemed like an impawssible undertaking. I was sure that everymouse would think I'd bitten off more cheese than I could chomp. Or worse, that I had CHEDDAR for brains."

Flora shook her snout, but I agreed with Randall. His experiment sounded like a fantasy!

He continued with his story. "I started collecting ORGANIC FOOD WASTE for my experiments. But I really needed an ENORMOUSE quantity, so I got myself hired at the Experimental Recycling Plant. I

figured that once I was there, I could quietly take some for my own research."

Hercule glanced over at Randall's STRANGE vehicle. "And this odd contraption? How did you make it?"

Randall's snout LIT UP for the first time since we had begun talking. "This BLIMP is entirely constructed from recycled plastic! It's the only vehicle of its kind in the world! I call it Air Bott. I'm still refining the construction. I have to keep a lot of plastic bottles on hand to make repairs."

Ah! That explained all the plastic bottles at the crime scene. "You should really be more careful with all those plastic bottles," I said. "We found them littering all the places you took garbage from!"

Thea walked around Air Bott, taking lots of pictures. "This is incredimouse!" she squeaked. Randall explained how the Air Bott worked, while I took lots of **notes**. This would make an excellent article for the *Gazette*!

# Air Bott

## RANDALL CRUMB'S MASTERPIECE

The name **Bott** is short for Bottle! **Randall Crumb** built it in his secret laboratory, on the outskirts of **New Mouse City**.

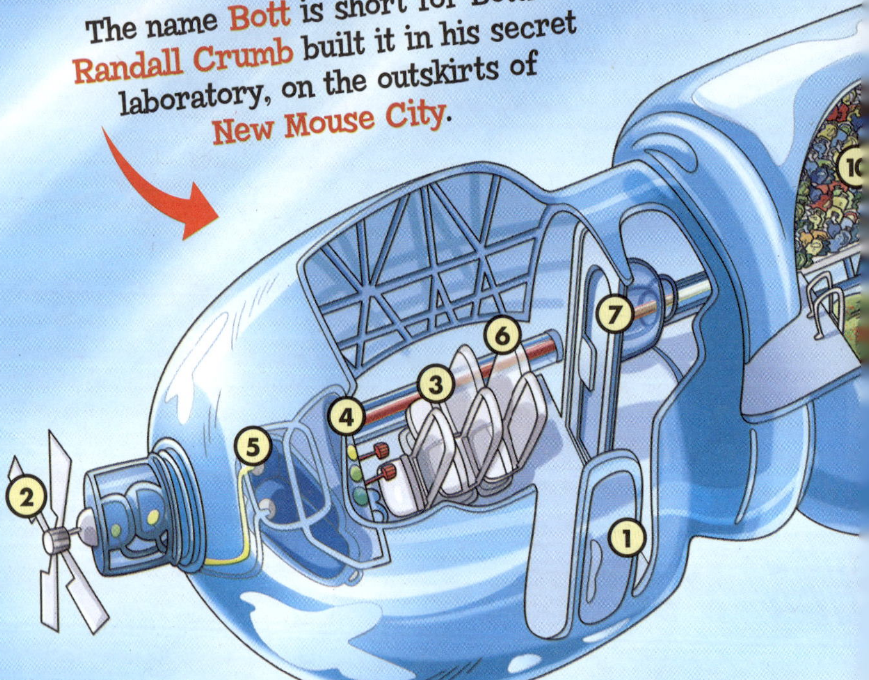

Please note that Randall only conducts his thefts when there is a full moon, otherwise he would not have enough energy to charge the Air Bott's batteries.

## LEGEND

Flying vehicle in the shape of an enormouse bottle. It was built using thousands and thousands of recycled plastic bottles.

1. MAIN DOOR
2. The PROPELLERS are made of plastic from bottle caps.
3. The SEATS were also built using recycled plastic from bottle caps.
4. The colorful CONTROL PANEL—it's made of various colors of soda bottles.
5. THE VEHICLE BATTERY is powered by moonlight, instead of the sun.
6. THE MAIN CABIN can hold up to five passengers, including the pilot.
7. THE INSULATED DOOR blocks the smell of the collected trash.
8. THE TRASH COMPARTMENT is used to load and dump the trash.
9. Reinforced transparent PLASTIC WING
10. Supply of PLASTIC BOTTLES for emergency repairs.
11. EXTERNAL DOOR

# ? TOP SECRET TRASH

When Randall finished explaining how the **Air Bott** worked, Hercule had even more questions.

"I'm dying to see how the trash recycling machine works! Will you show us?"

Randall finally **smiled** a little. "I'd actually love to show you how it works," he said. "Come with me." He waved his paw, and we followed him.

We put on **HELMETS** that had been made out of the same recycled plastic as Randall's. "Okay, then full speed ahead, to **GREENHILL**!" he cried, and turned the Air Bott's engines on.

After a few minutes in *flight*,

we finally arrived at a deserted area on top of a very **GREEN** hill near New Mouse City. I spotted a shed that looked like it had been abandoned for a **thousand** years.

Randall pressed a button on the control panel, and the shed's **ROOF** opened up.

Slowly, the Air Bott lowered inside the shed and touched down right in the middle

of the lab. Overhead, the shed roof closed itself back up with a hiss. Randall took his helmet off and grinned. "Welcome to my secret lab! It's well hidden, don't you think?"

Thea nodded her snout. "I don't think anymouse would think there was anything interesting inside this RATTY old shed," she agreed.

After we stowed our helmets and climbed out of the Air Bott, Randall showed us around his facility.

Soon, we came to a room full of computer monitors. I noticed that they all seemed to be old models. Randall nodded when he saw me examining the computers. "I would love to keep myself updated on every recycling research project in the world, but I need newer and more advanced computers. Some things I can't make myself

**RANDALL CRUMB'S LABORATORY**

1. RANDALL CRUMB'S OFFICE
2. LIBRARY (ALL THE BOOKS ARE ABOUT RECYCLING)
3. RANDALL'S APARTMENT
4. COMPUTER LAB
5. LABORATORY AND TRASH STORAGE (SEPARATED FROM THE LAB TO KEEP THE TRASH SMELL FROM SPREADING)

out of trash!"

When we arrived at Randall's **APARTMENT**, we had a simple but tasty **breakfast**.

Afterward, Randall finally took us to see what we had been waiting for: the trash recycling machine!

In his lab, behind a thick plastic wall rose the **ENORMOUSE** machine. "Great gobs of mozzarella," I cried. The machine was **STRANGELY** beautiful.

Made of transparent plastic, the contraption had an opening at the top for **trash**. Coming out of the machine there was an **electric** wire, connected to a light bulb. An incredimouse amount of **trash** had been piled all around it. Gnats **buzzed** everywhere. It must **SMELL** worse than a moldy pack of cheese sticks in there, but thankfully, the plastic wall kept the **SMELL** in with the machinc.

**But how did it work? I couldn't wait to see!**

# Florax!

Randall walked to a **command** panel full of **buttons**. "Are you ready to see how my recycling machine works? I have called it **FLORAX**, as an ode to all Flora's hard work in the field of recycling science!"

Flora **SMILED**. "Thanks, Randall!"

He turned a few knobs and pressed five or six **buttons**. Then, using a mechanical arm, he lifted some **trash** and dropped it into the machine. **FLORAX** let out a little burp: **burpppp!**

Randall's whiskers trembled. I could tell this demonstration must mean a lot to him. He'd never shown anyone his **TOP SECRET** work before!

Randall turned to us. "Ready?" he asked.

"We are!" we all **squeaked** together.

"Okay, then," he said. "One, two, three, goooo!" He pulled the **large** lever in the center of the command panel with all his mouse might. A loud **buzzing** sound filled the lab.

A **LIGHT BULB** on the top of Florax went on for a moment, gave a short **spark** of light . . . and then it went off again, with a sad ***SWOOSH*** sound!

1

Randall pulls the largest lever down.

2

The light bulb is on for a short moment.

3

The light bulb goes off.

Randall turned to us. "So that's all the energy I've been able to generate so far." He still looked anxious.

There was silence in the lab.

Next to me, I heard Hercule mumble, "That's it?!"

Randall's fur blushed PINK. "Well, uh, yes. That's it — for now! It turns out I have a problem. You need an ENORMOUSE quantity of trash to generate even a very small amount of energy! As you can see, all that trash was used to light up the LIGHT BULB for a very short time."

I put my PAW on Randall's shoulder. "You've still done a great job. It took an incredimouse amount of time and science to get that little light! You generated energy from trash! It makes me hopeful for the future of our planet!"

Thea nodded. “Randall, you’ve done great work here. But it doesn’t seem like a very practical machine in its current state. You would need a **HUGE** volume of trash to power even this small workshop.”

Randall lowered his snout, looking sad. “I know! That’s why I’ve kept my work a secret for so long. I’m stuck on how to improve the technology. Maybe I’m just not

good enough . . . I stole all that trash and caused so much trouble. I'm really sorry." He wrung his paws.

My heart squeaked for him. He had gotten so far. He couldn't give up now! I turned to my friends. "Well, he shouldn't have taken all that trash without asking. It did cause a lot of trouble. But finding new sources of energy is so important. I'm sure Mayor Fuzzypaws will understand."

Hercule looked thoughtful. "I assume what you need most is a lot of MONEY to pursue this research, right? And a more high-tech facility?"

Randall nodded. "Unfortunately, I have just about spent all my **savings** to get even this far. But I have always DREAMED of inventing truly clean energy. I am willing to give it all I have to make this a reality!"

Flora's snout LIT UP with a GIANT smile. "We will help you, Randall! And this amazing dream of yours? We will make it come true . . . together!"

"Mouse hug!" Hercule yelled, and pulled us all in for a group hug.

# Today's Trash, Tomorrow's Dream!

Flora was the first one to come forward with her offer. "The Experimental Recycling Plant's complete **ARCHIVE** will be available to Randall, as well as my own personal one. I hope they will be **helpful** in his research!"

Thea **CLAPPED** her paws together. "I have an **idea**! I will set up a **fundraiser** to benefit Randall. *The Rodent's Gazette* can be the sponsor and host. That way, we can take his cause to a wider audience!"

Hercule rubbed a paw over his **WHISKERS**. Finally, his eyes brightened. "Shredded cheddar with sour cream on the side! I have a fabumouse **idea**!"

Without explaining further, he pulled out his bananaphone and started dialing.

"Hello? Beaker? It's Hercule, your cousin. Are you in your lab? I would like you to meet an incredimouse young scientist. He's an inventor . . . He loves nature as much as you do . . ."

Hercule hung up the phone and turned back to us. "We need to raise funds for Randall, but connections in the scientific community are just as important! I will introduce him to my cousin Beaker, who runs the most MODERN and high-tech lab in New Mouse City!"

"Who needs sleep? Let's go right now!" Randall cried.

Hercule called the BANANAMOBILE to the secret lab. Once it arrived, we all hopped in and headed to Beaker's compound.

When we walked into Beaker's facility, we were breathless. It was an AMAZINGLY MODERN LAB with all the latest scientific tools!

Beaker warmly welcomed Randall. "It's so good to have you here, dear colleague! Hercule has told me all about you. I'd love for us to join forces. I know that with your research and my facilities, we can do great things!"

Randall teared up. "How marvemouse.

I would love that. Thank you, my dear friends! I will be worthy of your trust in me, I promise. I will do my best to perform mouserific work and get fabumouse results."

Suddenly, a little voice let out a squeak. "Geronimo, I missed you! I can't wait to go home!"

It was a small green computer, my beloved **CompStar**!

I scooped up CompStar and **hugged** it tight: "I missed you, too, CompStar! I can't wait to **work** together again!"

We will achieve great things!
Unbelievable technology!

What a fabumouse lab!
BEAKERUS POIRAT'S LAB

# A Visit from Creepella

Now that the mystery of the disappearing trash had been solved, everything was back to normal. I returned to my office, but I often found myself thinking about Randall and Flora, and their passion for environmental research.

Thea suggested that I find a way to share their scientific knowledge with our newspaper readers. I agreed that it was a mouserific idea, so I invited Flora into *The Rodent's Gazette* offices.

When she arrived, she had tons of ideas about how to make the science of recycling more accessible to the average mouse.

"Together we will help your readers understand how **important** it is to protect the environment, not only here on Mouse Island, but also on the whole **planet**! What a fabumouse **idea** you had for us to collaborate!"

"Well, really it was Thea's idea. But I will tell her you said so!" I said.

Together we **brainstormed** a few different articles she could write for the *Gazette*.

A few days later, she returned with an environmental supplement she had created with Randall's help.

"I hope it's the kind of thing you were looking for," Flora said.

# A NEW LIFE FOR OLD PLASTIC

## CREATIVE WAYS TO REUSE PLASTIC BOTTLES

### BIRD FEEDER

Have a grown-up help you poke some holes through a plastic bottle. Insert wooden spoons through the holes. Then fill the bottle with birdseed and hang it from a tree. The local birds will love your passion for recycling!

### DESSERT MOLD

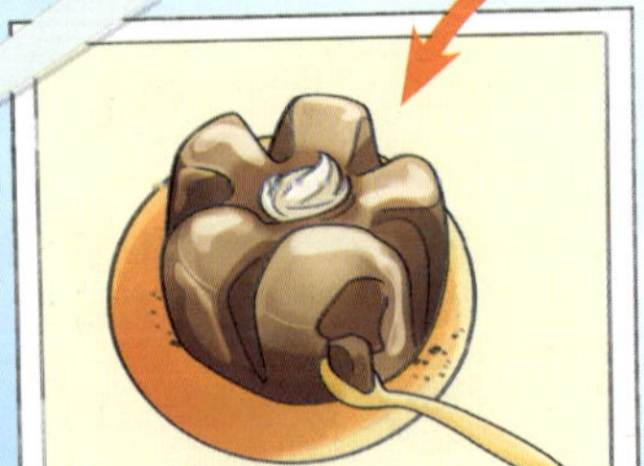

The bottom of any plastic bottle can be used to shape pudding. Mix it according to the package directions, then pour it into the bottom of a clean plastic soda bottle. After chilling, set your mo in warm water to help release the pudding from the mold.

**ALWAYS ASK AN ADULT FOR HELP**

## OBJECT HOLDER

In the upper part of a plastic bottle, cut out a round hole that's big enough for a hand. Gently sand the edges of the hole with sandpaper if they are sharp. Attach a hook on the bottle cap so you can hang it wherever you want. You can fill the bottles with objects that you love: a rock collection, coins, beads, buttons, etc.

## VERTICAL VEGETABLE GARDEN

Cut a large rectangle on the side of a bottle. Punch four holes in the bottle: one next to each of the four corners. Fill your bottle halfway with potting soil and the plant of your choice. Then insert a string through the holes and tie a secure knot in each. Now your planter is ready to hang!

ALWAYS ASK AN ADULT FOR HELP

## FLOWER VASE

Cut a plastic bottle in half and decorate the bottom half however you want. Then turn the top part of the bottle, with cap still screwed on tight, upside down and insert it in the lower part. Now your vase is ready for water and the flowers of your choice!

## BOWLING PINS

Empty plastic bottles can be used as bowling pins. Just set up empty plastic bottles in a V formation. Take turns with friends throwing a small soft ball at the plastic pins.

## PENCIL HOLDER

Cut a bottle at a height that you need. Then use sandpaper to smooth the cut edge so that it's no longer sharp. Now just add pencils!

## A BROOM

Cut off the bottom of a two-liter plastic bottle. Then cut vertical strips up to the top, all around the bottle. Next, insert a stick in the bottle neck and tie it up with a string or duct tape. Time for cleanup!

"I'm sure it's mouserific!" I squeaked.

"This is amaze-mouse, Flora!" I cried.

Just then the door to my office flew open, and Creepella stomped in with her long dark hair swishing around her shoulders.

"I thought I heard voices in here! Who is this?" Creepella asked.

Squeak!

"Creepella, this is Flora Fontal, head scientist over at the Experimental Recycling Plant," I explained. "She was just here to give me this article she wrote for the paper.

Flora turned around, and suddenly, both she and Creepella looked shocked!

"Cream cheese on toast!" Creepella said.

"Oh my cheddar muffins!" Flora said.

"It's Flora!" Creepella shouted.

"It's Creepella!" Flora shouted.

The two mice squeaked, ran toward each

other, and **hugged** tightly.

What in the name of Brie was going on?!

The two rodents turned toward me, their eyes **shining** with happiness.

"We were **best** friends in school," Flora explained.

"But then Flora moved away and we lost touch," Creepella said.

"I'm so **happy** to see you! You have to tell me everything that happened in your life after you left here!" Creepella said.

"You too!" Flora said. They shared a **laugh**.

"I couldn't be **happier** to find Flora here in your offices today," Creepella said,

smiling. "But I might need to steal her away from your important meeting for a cream cheese latte!"

Before I could object, Flora **happily** agreed. The two of them were out the door together so ***FAST***, I didn't even have a chance to say good-bye.

I sat back down in the **Peace** and quiet to work on my fondue article. Melted cheese doesn't write about itself! But that was short lived.

"Geronimo, you old **stinky** cheese!" came a shout, and Hercule's trademark **YELLOW** hat poked around my office door. He **bounded** inside. "I just saw Flora and Creepella. Apparently they're very old friends!"

I nodded. "Hercule, I really need to get back to this —"

"Creepella was telling some story about you, and they were LAUGHING and LAUGHING." His eyes twinkled.

I groaned. "Can I help you with something? Or did you just drop by to tease me?"

Hercule dropped into the chair next to my desk. "I just came by to make an EPIC suggestion! I think you should write up our trash adventure as a mystery thriller. With me as the handsome hero, of course. It would be entertaining — and teach readers about the importance of recycling!"

I rolled my eyes. But it wasn't a TERRIBLE idea . . .

"Just think about it!" Hercule said. He tipped his hat to me, stood, and then quickly

**dashed** back the way he'd come.

A mystery, hmm. That could be something. We had learned so much about recycling, and there was so much interesting information I could include. I flipped open **CompStar**, freshly back from being repaired.

**CompStar** let out several happy **BEEPS**. "Hello, Geronimo! Should I open that fondue article for you? I think you had just started writing about the eighth-best melted cheese restaurant in New Mouse City."

"Not just yet, CompStar! I have something else I want to work on. I'd like to open a *fresh* document, please!"

"A *fresh* document! How exciting!" CompStar beeped. "I've so missed working with you!"

I smiled. "I've **missed** working with you, too! It's good to have you back."

I started typing and didn't stop until I had written the whole thing. And . . . as I am sure you know by now, the mystery I wrote is the book that you are holding in your paws right now!

## Did you like it?

I hope so! I put my whole **heart** into it. Or as CompStar would say, "**BEEP, BEEP, BEEP!**"

# Don't miss a single fabumouse adventure!

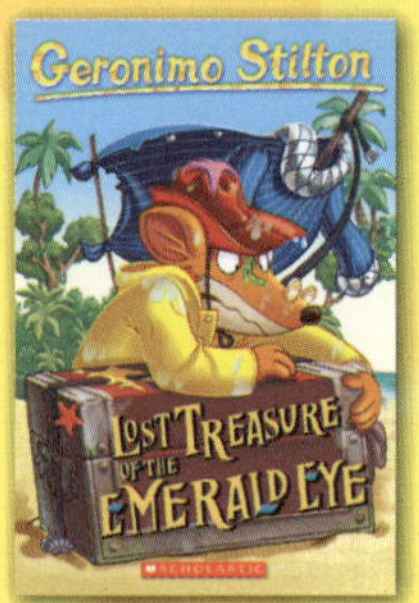

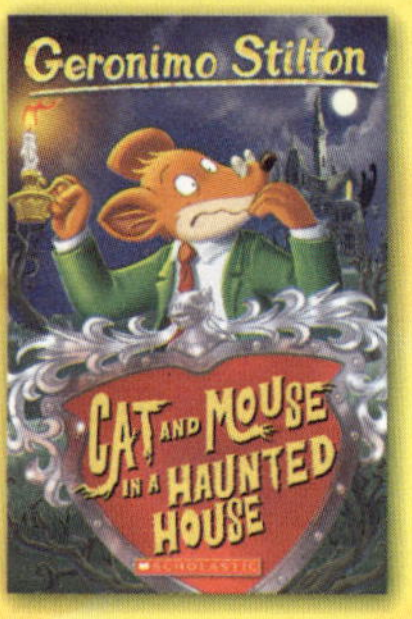

- #1 Lost Treasure of the Emerald Eye
- #2 The Curse of the Cheese Pyramid
- #3 Cat and Mouse in a Haunted House
- #4 I'm Too Fond of My Fur!
- #5 Four Mice Deep in the Jungle
- #6 Paws Off, Cheddarface!
- #7 Red Pizzas for a Blue Count
- #8 Attack of the Bandit Cats
- #9 A Fabumouse Vacation for Geronimo
- #10 All Because of a Cup of Coffee
- #11 It's Halloween, You 'Fraidy Mouse!
- #12 Merry Christmas, Geronimo!
- #13 The Phantom of the Subway
- #14 The Temple of the Ruby of Fire
- #15 The Mona Mousa Code
- #16 A Cheese-Colored Camper
- #17 Watch Your Whiskers, Stilton!
- #18 Shipwreck on the Pirate Islands
- #19 My Name Is Stilton, Geronimo Stilto
- #20 Surf's Up, Geronimo!
- #21 The Wild, Wild West
- #22 The Secret of Cacklefur Castle
- A Christmas Tale
- #23 Valentine's Day Disaster
- #24 Field Trip to Niagara Falls
- #25 The Search for Sunken Treasure
- #26 The Mummy with No Name
- #27 The Christmas Toy Factory
- #28 Wedding Crasher
- #29 Down and Out Down Under

- #30 The Mouse Island Marathon
- #31 The Mysterious Cheese Thief
- Christmas Catastrophe
- #32 Valley of the Giant Skeletons
- #33 Geronimo and the Gold Medal Mystery
- #34 Geronimo Stilton, Secret Agent
- #35 A Very Merry Christmas
- #36 Geronimo's Valentine
- #37 The Race Across America
- #38 A Fabumouse School Adventure
- #39 Singing Sensation
- #40 The Karate Mouse
- #41 Mighty Mount Kilimanjaro
- #42 The Peculiar Pumpkin Thief
- #43 I'm Not a Supermouse!
- #44 The Giant Diamond Robbery
- #45 Save the White Whale!
- #46 The Haunted Castle
- #47 Run for the Hills, Geronimo!
- #48 The Mystery in Venice
- #49 The Way of the Samurai
- #50 This Hotel Is Haunted!
- #51 The Enormouse Pearl Heist
- #52 Mouse in Space!
- #53 Rumble in the Jungle
- #54 Get into Gear, Stilton!
- #55 The Golden Statue Plot
- #56 Flight of the Red Bandit
- #57 The Stinky Cheese Vacation
- #58 The Super Chef Contest
- #59 Welcome to Moldy Manor
- #60 The Treasure of Easter Island
- #61 Mouse House Hunter
- #62 Mouse Overboard!
- #63 The Cheese Experiment
- #64 Magical Mission
- #65 Bollywood Burglary
- #66 Operation: Secret Recipe
- #67 The Chocolate Chase
- #68 Cyber-Thief Showdown
- #69 Hug a Tree, Geronimo
- #70 The Phantom Bandit
- #71 Geronimo on Ice!
- #72 The Hawaiian Heist
- #73 The Missing Movie
- #74 Happy Birthday, Geronimo!
- #75 The Sticky Situation
- #76 Superstore Surprise
- #77 The Last Resort Oasis
- #78 Mysterious Eye of the Dragon
- #79 Garbage Dump Disaster

**Up Next:**

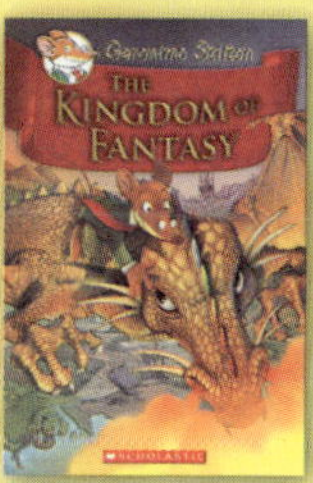


THE KINGDOM OF FANTASY

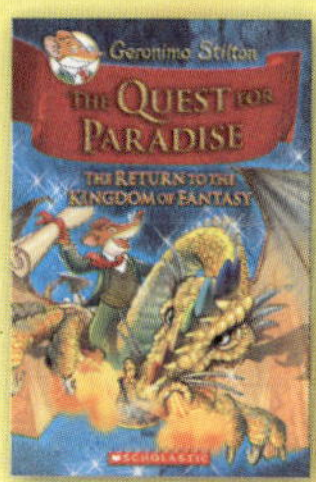


THE QUEST FOR PARADISE:
THE RETURN TO THE KINGDOM OF FANTASY

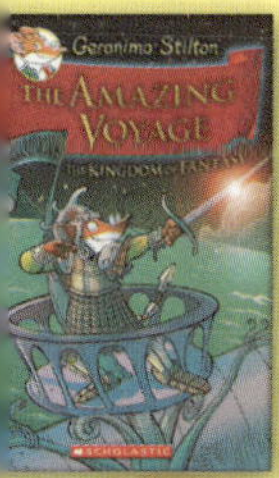


HE AMAZING VOYAGE:
E THIRD ADVENTURE IN THE KINGDOM OF FANTASY

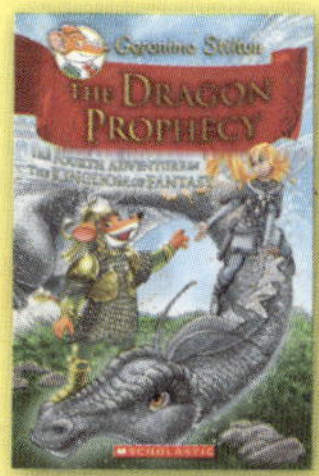


THE DRAGON PROPHECY:
THE FOURTH ADVENTURE IN THE KINGDOM OF FANTASY

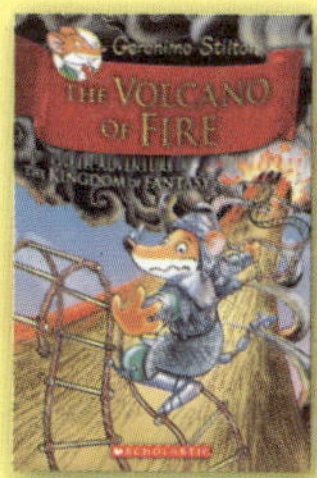


THE VOLCANO OF FIRE:
THE FIFTH ADVENTURE IN THE KINGDOM OF FANTASY

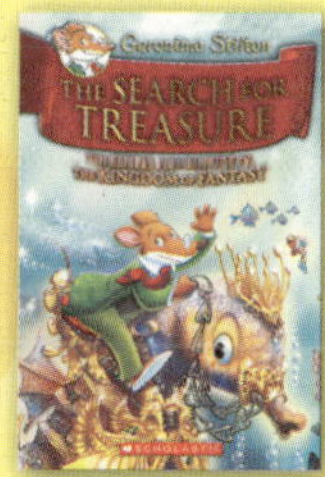


THE SEARCH FOR TREASURE:
THE SIXTH ADVENTURE IN THE KINGDOM OF FANTASY

THE ENCHANTED CHARMS:
THE SEVENTH ADVENTURE IN THE KINGDOM OF FANTASY

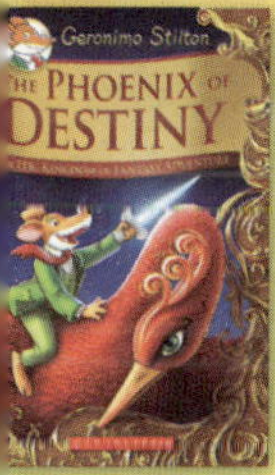


HE PHOENIX OF DESTINY:
I EPIC KINGDOM OF NTASY ADVENTURE

THE HOUR OF MAGIC:
THE EIGHTH ADVENTURE IN THE KINGDOM OF FANTASY

THE WIZARD'S WAND:
THE NINTH ADVENTURE IN THE KINGDOM OF FANTASY

THE SHIP OF SECRETS:
THE TENTH ADVENTURE IN THE KINGDOM OF FANTASY

THE DRAGON OF FORTUNE:
AN EPIC KINGDOM OF FANTASY ADVENTURE

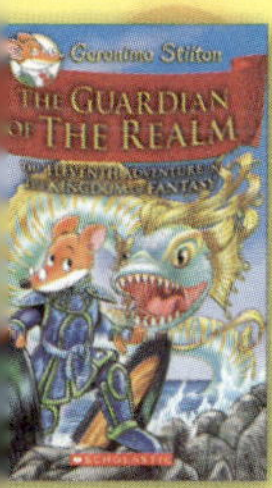


HE GUARDIAN F THE REALM:
THE ELEVENTH DVENTURE IN THE NGDOM OF FANTASY

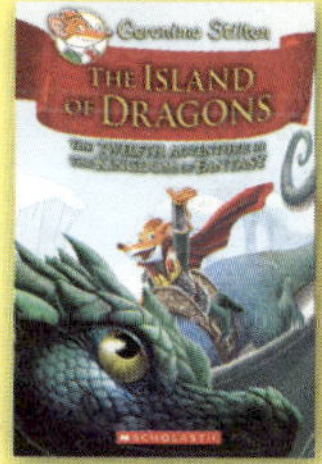


THE ISLAND OF DRAGONS:
THE TWELFTH ADVENTURE IN THE KINGDOM OF FANTASY

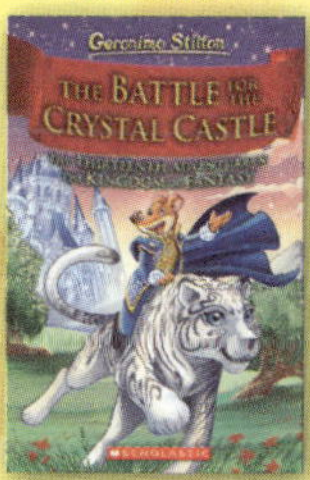


THE BATTLE FOR THE CRYSTAL CASTLE:
THE THIRTEENTH ADVENTURE IN THE KINGDOM OF FANTASY

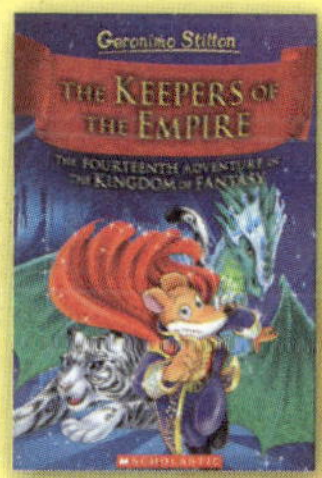


THE KEEPERS OF THE EMPIRE:
THE FOURTEENTH ADVENTURE IN THE KINGDOM OF FANTASY

# Don't miss any of these exciting Thea Sisters adventures!

Thea Stilton and the Dragon's Code

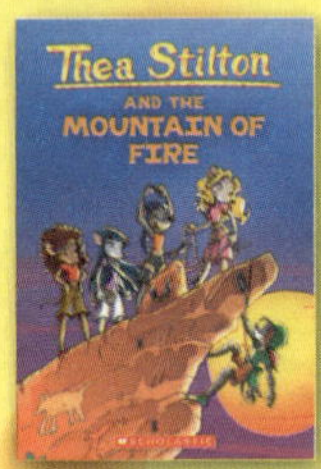


Thea Stilton and the Mountain of Fire

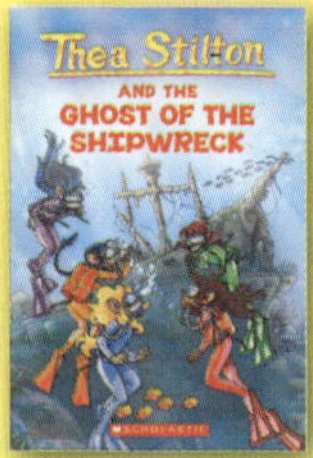


Thea Stilton and the Ghost of the Shipwreck

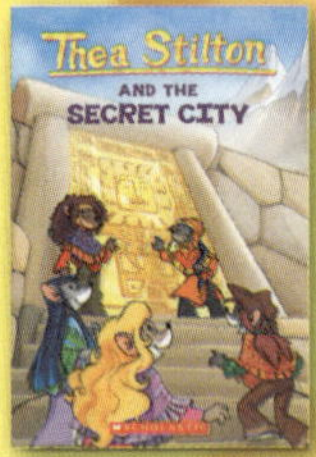


Thea Stilton and the Secret City

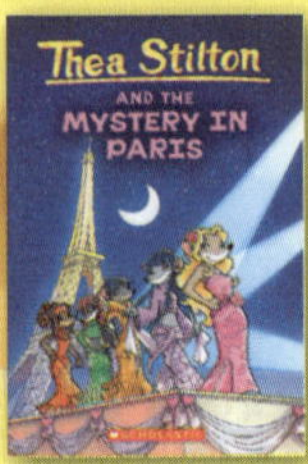


Thea Stilton and the Mystery in Paris

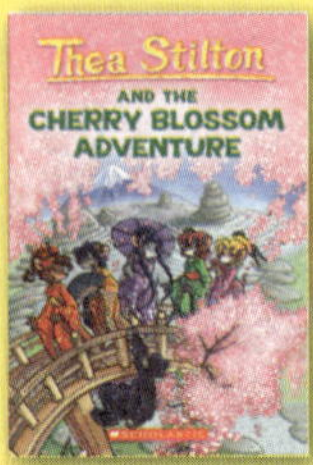


Thea Stilton and the Cherry Blossom Adventure

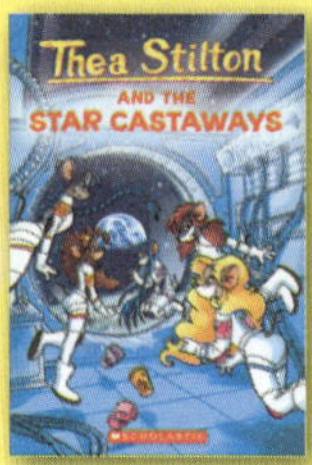


Thea Stilton and the Star Castaways

Thea Stilton: Big Trouble in the Big Apple

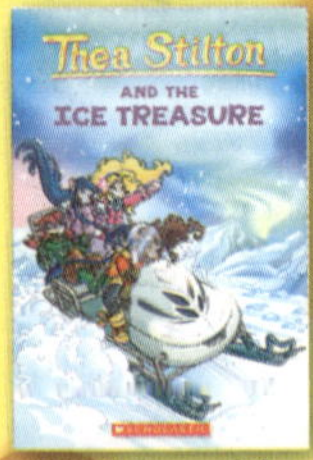


Thea Stilton and the Ice Treasure

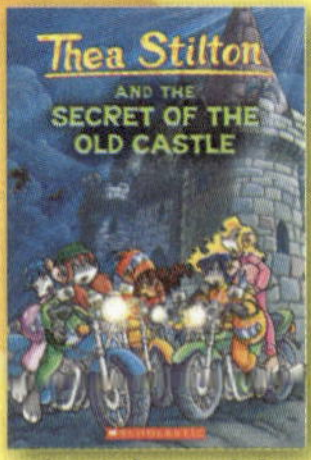


Thea Stilton and the Secret of the Old Castle

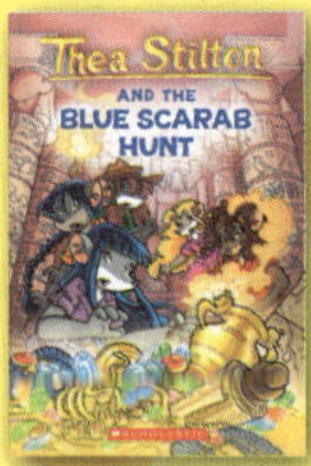


Thea Stilton and the Blue Scarab Hunt

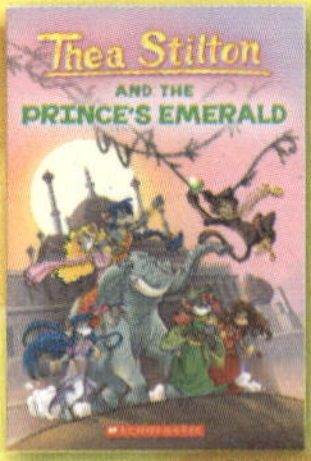


Thea Stilton and the Prince's Emerald

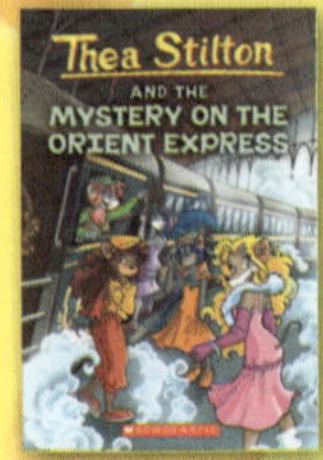


Thea Stilton and the Mystery on the Orient Express

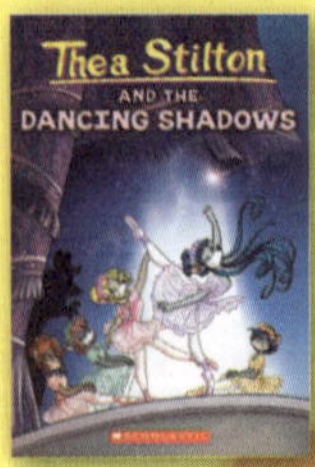


Thea Stilton and the Dancing Shadows

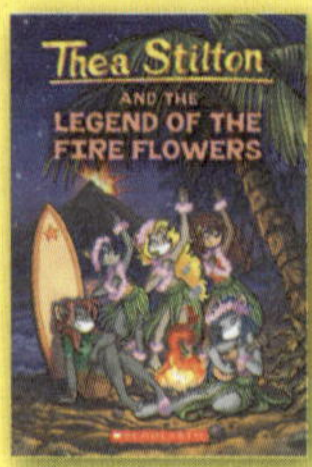


Thea Stilton and the Legend of the Fire Flowers

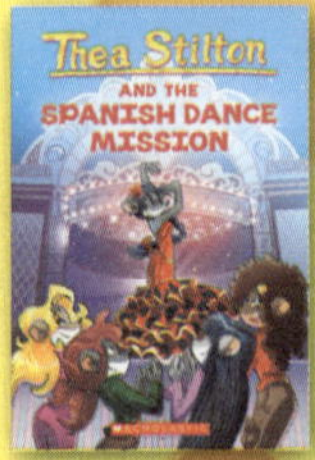


Thea Stilton and the Spanish Dance Mission

Thea Stilton and the Journey to the Lion's Den

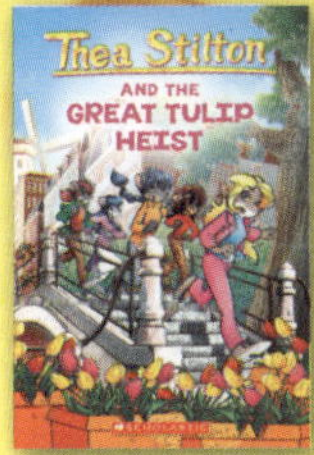

Thea Stilton and the Great Tulip Heist

Thea Stilton and the Chocolate Sabotage

Thea Stilton and the Missing Myth

Thea Stilton and the Lost Letters

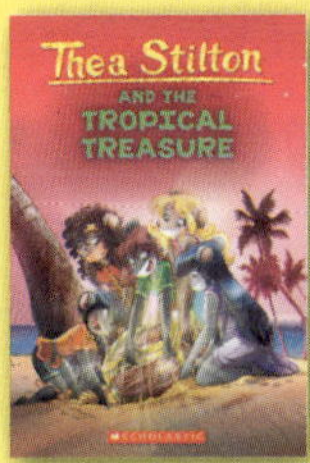

Thea Stilton and the Tropical Treasure

Thea Stilton and the Hollywood Hoax

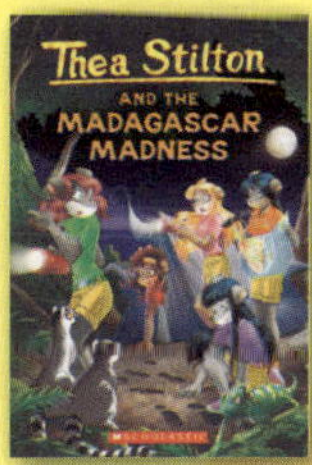

Thea Stilton and the Madagascar Madness

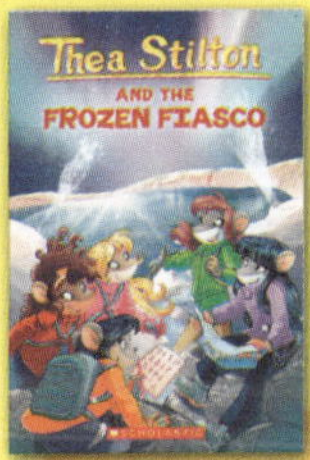

Thea Stilton and the Frozen Fiasco

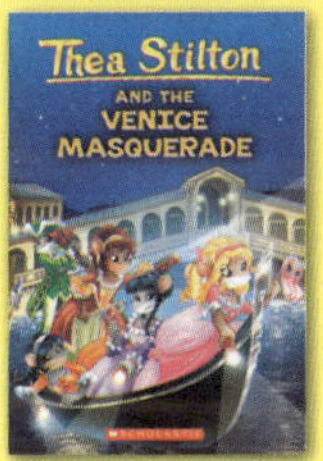

Thea Stilton and the Venice Masquerade

Thea Stilton and the Niagara Splash

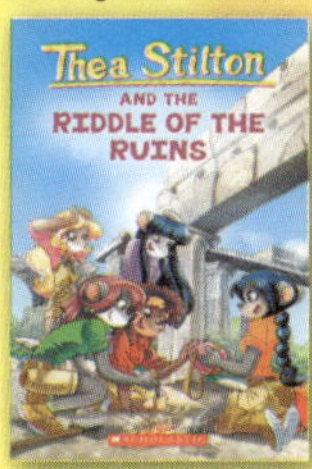

Thea Stilton and the Riddle of the Ruins

Thea Stilton and the Phantom of the Orchestra

Thea Stilton and the Black Forest Burglary

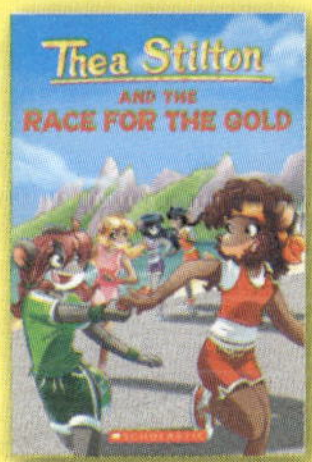

Thea Stilton and the Race for the Gold

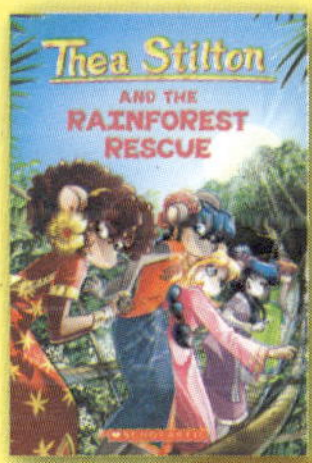

Thea Stilton and the Rainforest Rescue

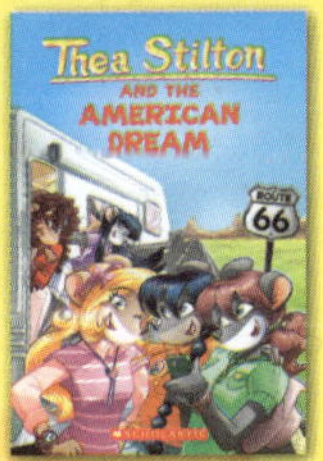

Thea Stilton and the American Dream

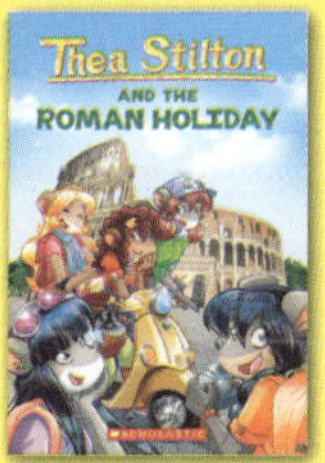

Thea Stilton and the Roman Holiday

1
2
3
4
5
6
7
8
9
10
11
12
13
14
15
16
17
18
19
20
21
22
23
24
25
26
27
28
29
30
31
32
33
34
35
36
37
38
39
40
41
42
43
44
45
46
RODENT
RIVER
Beach

# Map of New Mouse City

1. Industrial Zone
2. Cheese Factories
3. Angorat International Airport
4. WRAT Radio and Television Station
5. Cheese Market
6. Fish Market
7. Town Hall
8. Snotnose Castle
9. The Seven Hills of Mouse Island
10. Mouse Central Station
11. Trade Center
12. Movie Theater
13. Gym
14. Catnegie Hall
15. Singing Stone Plaza
16. The Gouda Theater
17. Grand Hotel
18. Mouse General Hospital
19. Botanical Gardens
20. Cheap Junk for Less (Trap's store)
21. Aunt Sweetfur and Benjamin's House
22. Mouseum of Modern Art
23. University and Library
24. *The Daily Rat*
25. *The Rodent's Gazette*
26. Trap's House
27. Fashion District
28. The Mouse House Restaurant
29. Environmental Protection Center
30. Harbor Office
31. Mousidon Square Garden
32. Golf Course
33. Swimming Pool
34. Tennis Courts
35. Curlyfur Island Amousement Park
36. Geronimo's House
37. Historic District
38. Public Library
39. Shipyard
40. Thea's House
41. New Mouse Harbor
42. Luna Lighthouse
43. The Statue of Liberty
44. Hercule Poirat's Office
45. Petunia Pretty Paws's House
46. Grandfather William's House

This way to the Rodent Straits
Brigand's Isle
Tomcat Island
Pirate Ship of Cats
Hamster Islands
Blue Dolphin Bay
Coral Reefs
This way to the Mousific Ocean
Stray Cat Harbor
San Mouscisco
Cat's Claw Bay
Panther Archipelago
Swissville
Cheddarton
Mouseport
This way to the Ratlantic Ocean
New Mouse City
Mousefort Beach
Furflung Island
This way to the Sea of Mice
N
W
E
S
MOUSE ISLAND
1
2
3
4
5
6
7
8
9
10
11
12
13
14
15
16
17
18
19
20
21
22
23
24
25
26
27
28
29
30
31
32
33
34
35
36
37

# Map of Mouse Island

1. Big Ice Lake
2. Frozen Fur Peak
3. Slipperyslopes Glacier
4. Coldcreeps Peak
5. Ratzikistan
6. Transratania
7. Mount Vamp
8. Roastedrat Volcano
9. Brimstone Lake
10. Poopedcat Pass
11. Stinko Peak
12. Dark Forest
13. Vain Vampires Valley
14. Goose Bumps Gorge
15. The Shadow Line Pass
16. Penny Pincher Castle
17. Nature Reserve Park
18. Las Ratayas Marinas
19. Fossil Forest
20. Lake Lake
21. Lake Lakelake
22. Lake Lakelakelake
23. Cheddar Crag
24. Cannycat Castle
25. Valley of the Giant Sequoia
26. Cheddar Springs
27. Sulfurous Swamp
28. Old Reliable Geyser
29. Vole Vale
30. Ravingrat Ravine
31. Gnat Marshes
32. Munster Highlands
33. Mousehara Desert
34. Oasis of the Sweaty Camel
35. Cabbagehead Hill
36. Rattytrap Jungle
37. Rio Mosquito

Dear mouse friends,
Thanks for reading, and farewell
till the next book.
It'll be another whisker-licking-good
adventure, and that's a promise!

Geronimo Stilton